CIVIL RIGHTS STORIES

Written by Anita Ganeri with illustrations by Toby Newsome

Published in 2026
by The Rosen Publishing Group, Inc.
2544 Clinton Street, Buffalo, NY 14224

First published in Great Britain in 2021 by Hodder and Stoughton

Editor: Amy Pimperton
Designer: Peter Scoulding
Cover design: Peter Scoulding
Illustrations: Toby Newsome
Page 2 photograph
© Adenike Oke

Cataloging-in-Publication Data

Names: Ganeri, Anita, author. | Newsome, Toby, illustrator.
Title: Racial equality / by Anita Ganeri, illustrated by Toby Newsome.
Description: Buffalo, NY : PowerKids Press, 2026. | Series: Civil rights stories | Includes glossary and index.
Identifiers: ISBN 9781499453737 (pbk.) | ISBN 9781499453744 (library bound) | ISBN 9781499453751 (ebook)
Subjects: LCSH:Racism--Juvenile literature. | Equality--Juvenile literature. | Race discrimination--Juvenile literature. | Minorities--Civil rights--Juvenile literature.
Classification: LCC HT1521.G364 2026 | DDC 305.8--dc23

Manufactured in the United States of America

CPSIA Compliance Information: Batch #CSPK26. For further information contact Rosen Publishing at 1-800-237-9932.

CONTENTS

WHAT IS RACIAL EQUALITY?

Everyone has the right to be equal. It doesn't matter what you look like or where you come from. You have the right to be treated in the same way as everybody else.

Racial equality is when everyone is treated the same, regardless of their race or skin color. Unfortunately, there are people who believe that they are better than others and treat them badly or unfairly. When this happens because of a person's race or the color of their skin, it is called racism.

In many countries today, racism is banned by law. It is against the law to insult, harm, or discriminate against a person because of their race or skin color.

Many people around the world campaigned for years to get these laws, often putting their own lives at risk.

Sometimes, these laws are broken or ignored. Not everyone gets the racial equality they deserve. There have been many breakthroughs, but there is still racism today.

SKIN COLOR AND PREJUDICE

Since ancient times, false ideas about skin color have influenced how people are treated. People with lighter skin were often believed to be more powerful, more important, and more beautiful than those with darker skin. This white privilege is still in place today.

As white people began to trade with Africa and Asia in the 14th century, they bought, sold, and enslaved people from the countries they visited.

Starting in the 1750s, Britain controlled large parts of India. From the 1880s, European nations colonized (took over) parts of Africa (see pages 12–13). Some Europeans stereotyped people of color. They suggested that black and brown skin was a sign that someone was poor, uneducated, dirty, stupid, or dangerous. They believed that white skin was a sign of being rich, educated, clean, clever and pure.

Racist people still believe in some or all of these stereotypes today. Overcoming this prejudice is a key aim in the fight for racial equality.

A HOSTILE TAKEOVER

From the 15th century, white European settlers began arriving in the Americas. Almost from the start, the Europeans were hostile to the Native Americans, the people who had lived there for thousands of years. For Native Americans, the results were disastrous.

Millions of Native Americans were enslaved and millions more were killed by diseases brought by the settlers, such as measles and smallpox, to which they had no immunity. In the 19th century, fierce battles were fought as Europeans tried to seize Native American land in North America. Armed with traditional weapons, Native Americans stood little chance against the Europeans' guns.

Europeans saw the Native Americans as "wild" and "savages" who did not deserve equal rights. In 1830, U.S. President Andrew Jackson passed the Indian Removal Act. This law allowed the government to seize Native American lands and force people to move onto reservations that had poor soil, little water, and terrible weather.

The Native American struggle against racism continues. The 1968 Indian Bill of Rights, and later the American Indian Religious Freedom Act of 1978, brought some important breakthroughs, but not the right to own the land they live on. This means that, even today, many Native Americans struggle to escape the poverty of the reservations or get a decent education.

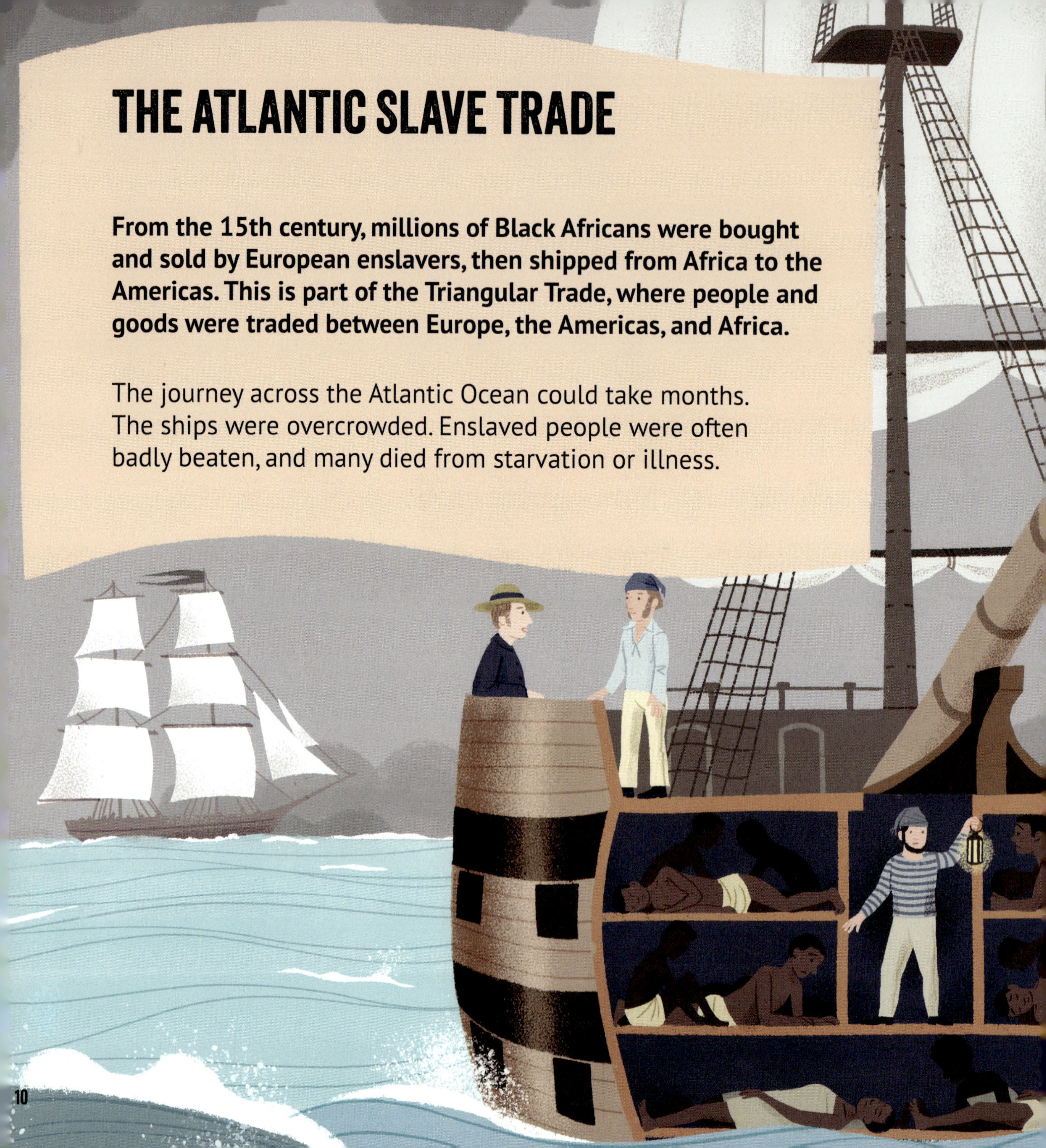

THE ATLANTIC SLAVE TRADE

From the 15th century, millions of Black Africans were bought and sold by European enslavers, then shipped from Africa to the Americas. This is part of the Triangular Trade, where people and goods were traded between Europe, the Americas, and Africa.

The journey across the Atlantic Ocean could take months. The ships were overcrowded. Enslaved people were often badly beaten, and many died from starvation or illness.

On arrival, enslaved people were sold at auction as if they were objects, not human beings. Then, they were made to work on plantations, growing crops such as sugar and cotton. These goods were shipped within the United States and to Europe as part of the Triangular Trade.

Enslaved people made their owners very rich, but their own lives were miserable. Enslaved people had no rights, had their names changed by their owners, and were not paid. They lived in terrible conditions and many died because of overwork. If they tried to run away, they were beaten or even murdered by their owners.

In 1807, the slave trade was banned in parts of the British Empire, including Australia and South Africa. Slavery itself was abolished in the British Empire in 1833. The Netherlands abolished slavery in 1863 and the United States in 1865, although freed slaves still faced many challenges.

THE "SCRAMBLE FOR AFRICA"

After the Atlantic Slave Trade was banned, white Europeans were still drawn to Africa for its gold, timber, rubber, and other riches. From the 1880s, countries including France, Britain, and Belgium took control of much of the continent. They raced to claim as much land as they could. They divided Africa between them. In some places, people from the same ethnic group were left stranded on different sides of new national boundaries.

At that time, most white Europeans thought they were better than Black people. All over Africa, missions were set up to convert Africans to Christianity, the Europeans' main religion.

White Europeans also forced Africans (and many Indian people who were made to go to Africa) to work very hard, harvesting crops and building roads and railroads. Those that rebelled or tried to resist were treated with violence and cruelty. Many were brutally murdered. The way Black and Asian people were thought of and treated at this time, compared with white people, is a part of why racism still exists today.

AUSTRALIA'S STOLEN LANDS

Mainland Australia's First Nations Peoples have lived on the continent for more than 50,000 years. They are thought to have sailed there from Asia, bringing their own culture and languages. For years, they have lived closely with the land, which they believe to be sacred.

Around 250 years ago, white British settlers came to Australia. They brought with them diseases that killed thousands of First Nations People.

Laws were passed that gave settlers the right to steal First Nations People's lands. The laws said, falsely, that the lands had been "empty," and so had belonged to no one. This law resulted in thousands of First Nations People being murdered for their lands.

In just 100 years, the numbers of First Nations People fell from around 1 million to 60,000.

Racist laws against First Nations People lasted well into the 20th century. From 1910 to 1970, the Australian government took thousands of First Nations children, by force, from their homes, and sent them to live with white families.

The children were not allowed to speak their own languages, and often had to change their names.

Racism against First Nations People continues in Australia today.

BRITAIN BY BOAT

On June 22, 1948, the HMT *Empire Windrush* sailed into Tilbury Docks, in Essex, England. On board were around 500 Black, British Commonwealth citizens from the West Indies.

Over the next 20 years, many more people arrived from the West Indies, and from India and Pakistan. Many had answered job ads and came to work in hospitals, hotels and restaurants. London Transport asked people in the Caribbean to come and work for them as bus conductors or station staff.

Far from being welcomed, the new arrivals were often called racist names and attacked. Many white landlords refused to rent rooms to Black and Asian people.

As more immigrants arrived, gangs of white racists took to the streets. In 1959, a Black man called Kelso Cochrane was stabbed to death by a white gang. His killers were never caught.

Kelso Cochrane

Over the years, *Windrush* immigrants have made a huge contribution to Britain. Despite this, racial inequality means that they have not always been treated well.

In 2018, the British government began deporting some of the *Windrush* people, and their families. The government wrongly accused them of not having documents to prove that they were allowed to live in the UK.

SEGREGATION IN THE USA

By the middle of the 20th century, Black people in the United States were still treated as second-class citizens. In many states, strict laws kept them apart from white people in places including schools and restaurants, and on public transportation. This is known as segregation.

On December 1, 1955, in Montgomery, Alabama, a Black woman named Rosa Parks refused to give up her seat on the bus for a white person. She was arrested and ordered to pay a fine. In protest, pastor and Black civil rights leader, Martin Luther King Jr. called for a boycott of the city's buses. The boycott was planned for one day only: Monday December 5th. It would take courage for Black people to see it through.

Rosa Parks

The bus boycott was a huge success and ended up lasting for over a year. Finally, on December 20, 1956, the order came from the U.S. Supreme Court to end bus segregation. The next day, Martin Luther King Jr. and other leaders rode on the city's first integrated bus.

THE POWER OF WORDS

After the Montgomery bus boycott, Martin Luther King Jr. continued the struggle for racial equality in the United States. He traveled around the country giving speeches, leading protest marches, and joining student sit-ins.

On August 28, 1963, some 250,000 people, both Black and white, marched through the U.S. capital, Washington, DC. They stopped in front of the Lincoln Memorial to listen to speeches from civil rights leaders.

Last to speak was Martin Luther King Jr. He talked about freedom and equal rights. In his famous "I Have a Dream ..." speech, he spoke about his hope that in the future people would not face prejudice based on the color of their skin.

The following year, the U.S. Congress passed the Civil Rights Act.

In April 1968, Martin Luther King Jr. arrived in Memphis, Tennessee, to march with the city's sanitation workers to demand better pay and working conditions. On the evening of April 4, he was shot on his motel balcony and died later in hospital. His killer was a known racist.

In August 2011, The Martin Luther King Jr. Memorial was completed to honor his work and legacy. This stone sculpture stands close to the Lincoln Memorial at 1964 Independence Avenue.

APARTHEID IN SOUTH AFRICA

From 1948 until the early 1990s, South Africa came under apartheid rule. Apartheid means "apartness" in Afrikaans (a language that is spoken in South Africa). Laws forced Black people and white people to live and work apart.

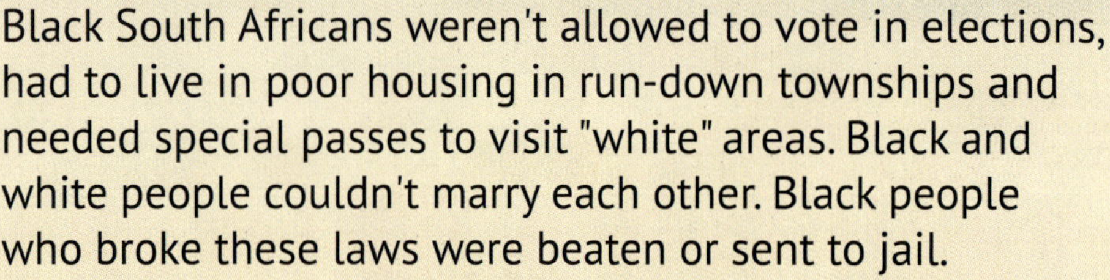

Black South Africans weren't allowed to vote in elections, had to live in poor housing in run-down townships and needed special passes to visit "white" areas. Black and white people couldn't marry each other. Black people who broke these laws were beaten or sent to jail.

In June 1976, thousands of students in Soweto, a Black township, protested against apartheid. Things turned violent and the police opened fire. More than 175 people were killed and thousands more injured.

In 1962, Nelson Mandela, a leader of the African National Congress (ANC), was arrested and sentenced to life imprisonment.

In 1990, after 27 years in prison, Mandela was released. He began talks with South Africa's white government to end apartheid. Four years later, elections were held in which all people of color were able to vote for the first time. The ANC won the election, and Mandela became South Africa's first Black president.

Nelson Mandela

CULTURE AND PREJUDICE

People of color have made huge contributions to culture, creating film, books, music, art, dance, television, and theater. Yet, there are far fewer opportunities for Black, Asian, and other artists of color to be represented in areas such as classical music, fine art, or ballet.

In recent years, the film world has been criticized for not having more diversity in directing or leading roles, nor rewarding Black actors for their work. In 2015 and 2016, no people of color were nominated for acting awards at the Academy Awards in the United States. In 2020, only one Black actor received an acting nomination.

There are now campaigns for greater diversity, and there have been some breakthroughs. In 2016, actor Chadwick Boseman, who sadly died in 2020, starred as the superhero Black Panther in the blockbuster *Black Panther*.

Boseman broke many stereotypes. He became one of very few Black leading actors who was given a leading Hollywood role. He gave Black people a Black superhero that they could identify with.

Chadwick Boseman

BLACK LIVES MATTER

Trayvon Martin

Black Lives Matter started as a civil rights movement in the United States. It was set up in 2013 by three Black women: Opal Tometi, Patrisse Cullors, and Alicia Garza.

Black Lives Matter was a response to the fatal shooting in Florida in 2012 of Black teenager Trayvon Martin. Trayvon was shot by George Zimmerman, who has Peruvian and white-German heritage. Prosecutors tried to show that this was a hate crime because Trayvon was Black, but Zimmerman was later found not guilty of murder or manslaughter.

Since 2013, Black Lives Matter protests and events have spread around the world to challenge racism and empower Black people.

In 2020, George Floyd, a Black man, was murdered in Minneapolis, Minnestoa, by a white police officer who knelt on his neck. His death was caught on camera and caused outrage across the world. Millions of people took part in Black Lives Matter protests, horrified by what had happened.

Black Lives Matter is so important because it shows that we do not yet have racial equality. Until we do, then we cannot say that all lives matter.

It is hoped that movements like Black Lives Matter will mark the beginning of real and lasting change in the struggle for racial justice and equality.

RACIAL EQUALITY TODAY

Today, there are laws giving everyone equal rights, regardless of skin color or race. Progress has been made, but laws and rights are sometimes ignored. Today, people of color are still facing discrimination and violence.

Racism means that Black, Asian, and other people of color are more likely to be stopped and searched by the police. Discrimination causes many Black children to be wrongly labeled as troublemakers at school. Racism means that if you have an "ethnic-sounding" name, you may be less likely to be offered a job.

Often white people refuse to see that they may be racist or are acting in a racist way. Because they are not affected by racism, some white people don't think carefully about their words and actions. They cause hurt and offense through ignorance. This is part of the problem and is a part of what is called white privilege.

Racism isn't a "Black" problem that is fixed by, for example, electing a Black person as the U.S. president. Racism is a problem that can only be solved by the majority of people working towards a common goal and actively being anti-racist.

RACIAL EQUALITY TIMELINE

Here is a list of moments in history found in this book that help to tell the story of the ongoing fight for racial equality.

1300s: Europeans trading with Asia and Africa buy and sell enslaved people along trade routes.

1492: White settlers arrive in the Americas, causing the deaths of millions of Native Americans.

1502: The Atlantic Slave Trade begins with the first enslaved Africans who were brought to Hispaniola by Spain. Millions of Black African men, women, and children are captured and forced into slavery. Many die or are murdered on the slave ships that transport them across the Atlantic.

1780s: White settlers begin to arrive in Australia. They steal land from First Nations Peoples, spread diseases, and kill thousands.

1807: Parts of the British Empire ban the slave trade.

1830: The Indian Removal Act forces Native Americans off their lands and onto reservations.

1833: The British Empire abolishes slavery.

1863: The Netherlands abolishes slavery.

1865: The United States abolishes slavery.

1877: Southern states introduce strict segregation laws (also known as the Jim Crow laws) for Black people.

1880s: Belgium, Britain, France, Germany, Italy, Portugal, and Spain exploit Africa's people and rich resources during the "Scramble for Africa."

1910–1970s: Thousands of First Nations children in Australia are stolen from their families.

1948: HMT *Empire Windrush* brings immigrants to Britain from the Commonwealth. New arrivals are treated with hostility.

1948–90s: South Africa comes under apartheid rule.

1955: Rosa Parks is arrested for refusing to give up her seat on a bus. It becomes an important moment in the fight for Black civil rights.

1962: Nelson Mandela is imprisoned.

1963: Martin Luther King Jr. leads many protest marches and makes many speeches, including his famous "I Have a Dream ..." speech on the Lincoln Memorial, in Washington, DC.

1964: U.S. Congress passes the Civil Rights Act.

1968: Martin Luther King Jr. is assassinated.

1968: In the United States, the Indian Bill of Rights is passed.

1976: More than 175 people are killed in the Soweto uprising, protesting over apartheid.

1978: In the United States, the American Indian Religious Freedom Act is passed. Native Americans are still denied the right to own the land they live on.

1990: Nelson Mandela is released.

1994: Nelson Mandela becomes South Africa's first Black president.

2008: Barack Obama becomes the first Black president of the United States.

2011: The Martin Luther King, Jr. Memorial sculpture is completed in Washington, DC.

2013: Black Lives Matter is set up in response to the shooting of Black teenager Trayvon Martin.

2018: The British government begins illegally deporting *Windrush*-generation families.

2020: George Floyd is murdered by a police officer kneeling on his neck. This sparks outrage and Black Lives Matter protests across the world.

GLOSSARY

abolish to formally end (in law)

boycott to refuse to buy or use something

civil rights the rights to equality and to political and social freedom

colonize to settle in a land and then control its people

Commonwealth a group of countries (many of which were part of the former British Empire); the Commonwealth of Nations

discriminate to treat people differently based on prejudice

empower to give someone the confidence or the power to do something

hate crime a crime motivated by prejudice based on, for example, someone's race or sex

hostile aggressive and unfriendly

ignorance a lack of knowledge

immigrant a person who goes to live in a country foreign to them

immunity protection from a deadly disease

landlord someone who owns or rents out land or buildings

measles an infectious disease that causes fever and a rash, and can cause death

mission Christians who are spreading the Christian religion; the buildings from which they spread their faith

plantation an estate where crops are grown

poverty the state of being extremely poor

prejudice dislike or hostility toward someone that is based on false ideas about that person

rebel to resist authority; to take action to oppose something

reservation an area of land set aside for a group of people, such as Native Americans

sanitation worker someone whose job is to take away trash

settler someone who moves to live in a new place along with others from the same group

smallpox an infectious disease that causes fever and skin lesions and can cause death

stereotype widely believed and often simplistic idea of what a person is like

Triangular Trade goods taken to Africa were traded for enslaved Africans, who were then shipped to the Americas. The products enslaved people produced there, such as sugar, rum, and cotton, were shipped back to Europe.

white privilege the advantages that white people have because they are not subject to racism in a society that discriminates against Black people and other people of color.

BOOKS TO READ

Children in Our World: Racism and Intolerance
by Louise Spilsbury and illustrated by Hanane Kai (Wayland, 2018)

Children in Our World: Rights and Equality
by Marie Murray and illustrated by Hanane Kai (Wayland, 2021)

Questions and Feelings About: Racism
by Anita Ganeri and illustrated by Ximena Jeria (Franklin Watts, 2020)

Info Buzz: Black History (series)
by various authors, (Franklin Watts, 2019)

INDEX